CONGRATULATIONS . . . . .

Welcome to the ranks of Cessna owners! Your Cessna has been designed
and constructed to give you the most in performance, economy, and com-
fort. It is our desire that you will find flying it, either for business or
pleasure, a pleasant and profitable experience.

This Owner's Manual has been prepared as a guide to help you get the
most pleasure and utility from your Model 150. It contains information
about your Cessna's equipment, operating procedures, and performance;
and suggestions for its servicing and care. We urge you to read it from
cover to cover, and to refer to it frequently.

Our interest in your flying pleasure has not ceased with your purchase of
a Cessna. World-wide, the Cessna Dealer Organization backed by the
Cessna Service Department stands ready to serve you. The following
services are offered by most Cessna Dealers:

> FACTORY TRAINED PERSONNEL to provide you with courteous
> expert service.
>
> FACTORY APPROVED SERVICE EQUIPMENT to provide you
> with the most efficient and accurate workmanship possible.
>
> A STOCK OF GENUINE CESSNA SERVICE PARTS on hand
> when you need them.
>
> THE LATEST AUTHORITATIVE INFORMATION FOR SERV-
> ICING CESSNA AIRPLANES, since Cessna Dealers have all
> of the Service Manuals and Parts Catalogs, kept current by
> Service Letters and Service News Letters, published by Cessna
> Aircraft Company.

We urge all Cessna owners to use the Cessna Dealer Organization to the
fullest.

A current Cessna Dealer Directory accompanies your new airplane. The
Directory is revised frequently, and a current copy can be obtained from
your Cessna Dealer. Make your Directory one of your cross-country
flight planning aids; a warm welcome awaits you at every Cessna Dealer.

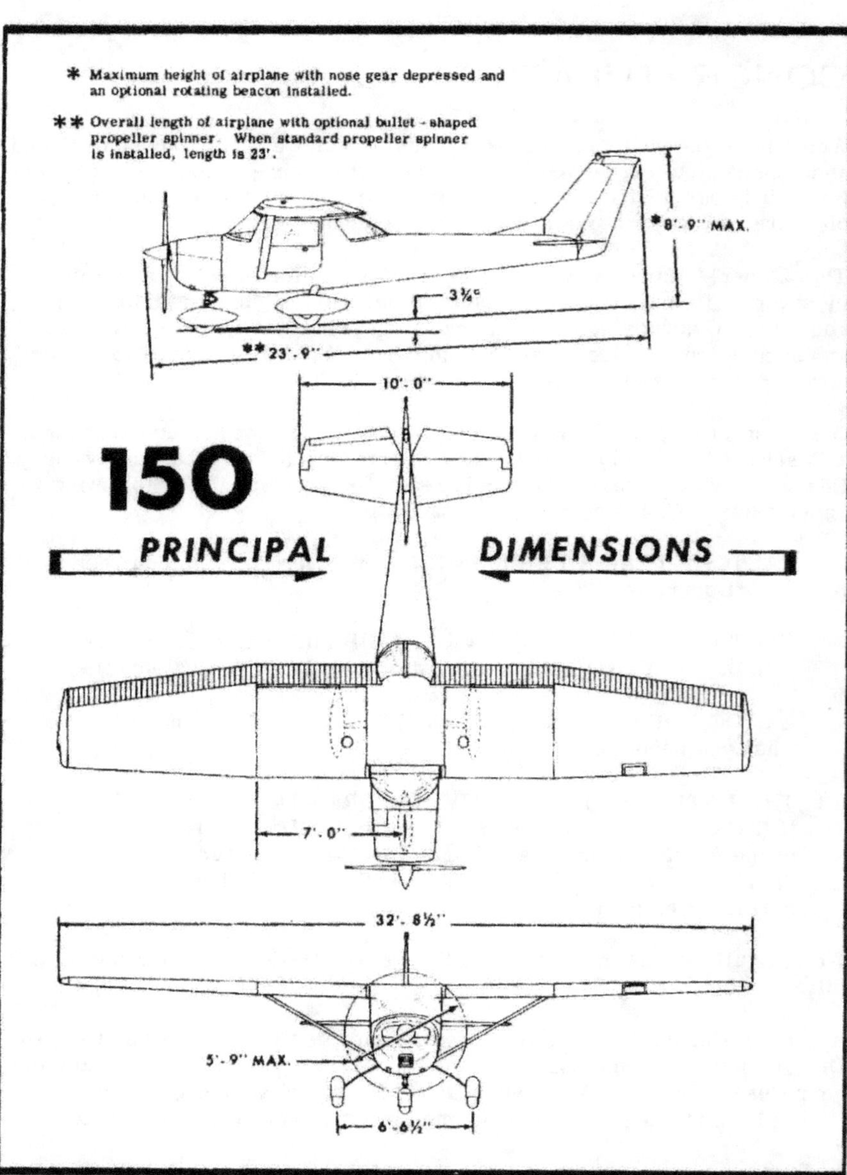

* Maximum height of airplane with nose gear depressed and an optional rotating beacon installed.
** Overall length of airplane with optional bullet - shaped propeller spinner. When standard propeller spinner is installed, length is 23'.
* 8'- 9" MAX.
3 ¼"
** 23'- 9"
10'- 0"
150
PRINCIPAL DIMENSIONS
7'- 0"
32'- 8½"
5'- 9" MAX.
6'- 6½"

PERFORMANCE - SPECIFICATIONS

IIII ONE FIFTY IIIIIIIIIIIIIIIIIIIIIIIIIIIIIIIIIIIIIIIIIII	STANDARD AND TRAINER	COMMUTER
GROSS WEIGHT	1600 lbs	1600 lbs
SPEED:		
Top Speed At Sea Level	123 mph	125 mph
Cruise, 75% Power at 7500 ft	120 mph	122 mph
RANGE:		
Cruise, 75% Power at 7500 ft	480 mi	490 mi
22.5 Gallons, No Reserve	4.0 hrs	4.0 hrs
	120 mph	122 mph
Cruise, 75% Power at 7500 ft	745 mi	760 mi
Long Range Version, 35.0 Gallons	6.2 hrs	6.2 hrs
	120 mph	122 mph
Optimum Range at 10,000 ft	560 mi	565 mi
22.5 Gallons, No Reserve	5.7 hrs	5.7 hrs
	98 mph	99 mph
Optimum Range at 10,000 ft	870 mi	885 mi
Long Range Version, 35.0 Gallons	8.9 hrs	8.9 hrs
	98 mph	99 mph
RATE OF CLIMB AT SEA LEVEL	670 fpm	670 fpm
SERVICE CEILING	12,650 ft	12,650 ft
TAKE-OFF:		
Ground Run	735 ft	735 ft
Total Distance Over 50-ft Obstacle . .	1385 ft	1385 ft
LANDING:		
Landing Roll	445 ft	445 ft
Total Distance Over 50-ft Obstacle . .	1075 ft	1075 ft

EMPTY WEIGHT: (Approximate)

	Standard	Trainer	COMMUTER
With Standard Fuel Tanks . . .	970 lbs	1000 lbs	1060 lbs
With Long Range Fuel Tanks . .	975 lbs	1005 lbs	1065 lbs

	STANDARD AND TRAINER	COMMUTER
BAGGAGE	120 lbs	120 lbs
WING LOADING: Pounds/Sq Foot	10.2	10.2
POWER LOADING: Pounds/HP.	16.0	16.0
FUEL CAPACITY:		
Total (Standard Tanks)	26 gal.	26 gal.
Total (Long Range Tanks)	38 gal.	38 gal.
OIL CAPACITY: Total	6 qts	6 qts
PROPELLER: Fixed Pitch (Diameter)	69 inches	69 inches
ENGINE: Continental Engine	O-200A	O-200A
100 rated HP at 2750 RPM		

TABLE OF CONTENTS

This manual describes the operation and performance of the Standard Model 150, the Commuter and the Trainer. Equipment described as "Optional" denotes that the subject equipment is optional on the Standard airplane. Much of this equipment is standard on the Commuter and Trainer.

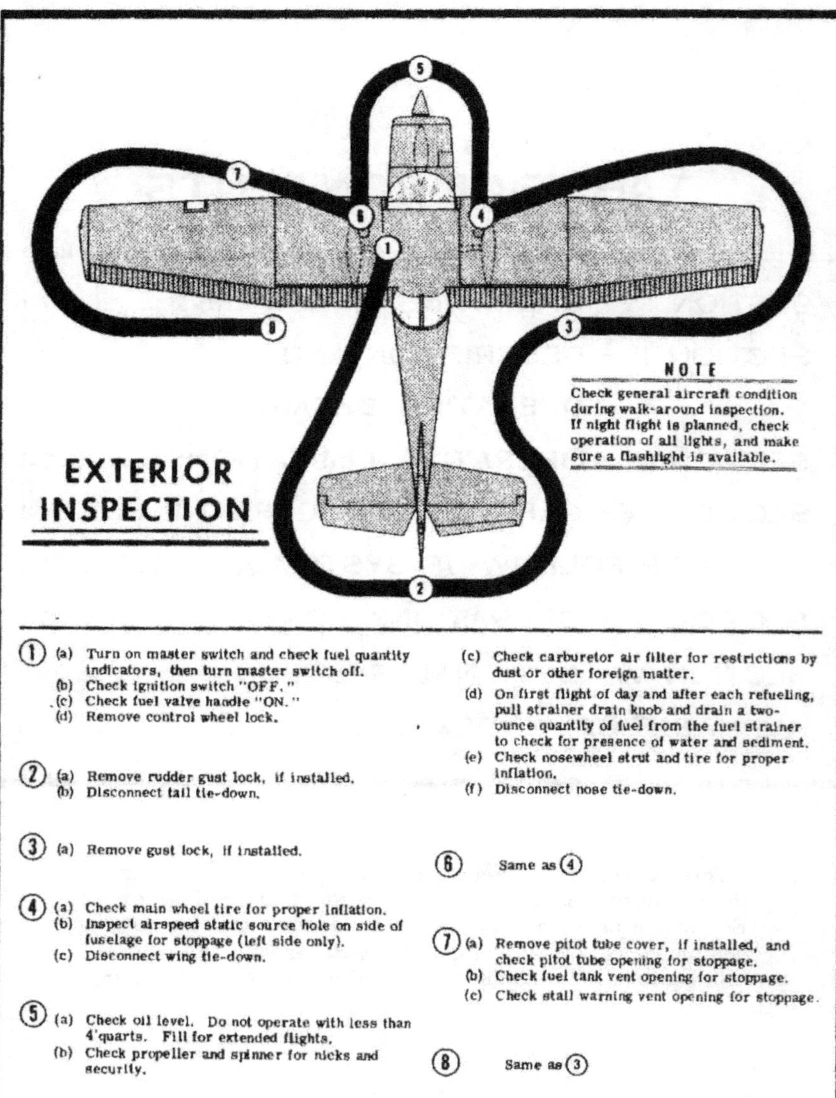

5
7
6
4
1
8
3
2
EXTERIOR INSPECTION
NOTE
Check general aircraft condition during walk-around inspection. If night flight is planned, check operation of all lights, and make sure a flashlight is available.
(1) (a) Turn on master switch and check fuel quantity indicators, then turn master switch off.
(b) Check ignition switch "OFF."
(c) Check fuel valve handle "ON."
(d) Remove control wheel lock.
(2) (a) Remove rudder gust lock, if installed.
(b) Disconnect tail tie-down.
(3) (a) Remove gust lock, if installed.
(4) (a) Check main wheel tire for proper inflation.
(b) Inspect airspeed static source hole on side of fuselage for stoppage (left side only).
(c) Disconnect wing tie-down.
(5) (a) Check oil level. Do not operate with less than 4 quarts. Fill for extended flights.
(b) Check propeller and spinner for nicks and security.
(c) Check carburetor air filter for restrictions by dust or other foreign matter.
(d) On first flight of day and after each refueling, pull strainer drain knob and drain a two-ounce quantity of fuel from the fuel strainer to check for presence of water and sediment.
(e) Check nosewheel strut and tire for proper inflation.
(f) Disconnect nose tie-down.
(6) Same as (4)
(7) (a) Remove pitot tube cover, if installed, and check pitot tube opening for stoppage.
(b) Check fuel tank vent opening for stoppage.
(c) Check stall warning vent opening for stoppage.
(8) Same as (3)

Figure 1-1.

OPERATING CHECK LIST

One of the first steps in obtaining the utmost performance, service, and flying enjoyment from your Cessna is to familiarize yourself with your airplane's equipment, systems, and controls. This can best be done by reviewing this equipment while sitting in the airplane. Those items whose function and operation are not obvious are covered in Section II.

Section I lists, in Pilot's Check List form, the steps necessary to operate your airplane efficiently and safely. It is not a check list in its true form as it is considerably longer, but it does cover briefly all of the points that you should know for a typical flight.

The flight and operational characteristics of your airplane are normal in all respects. There are no unconventional characteristics or operations that need to be mastered. All controls respond in the normal way within the entire range of operation. All airspeeds mentioned in Sections I and II are indicated airspeeds. Corresponding calibrated airspeeds may be obtained from the Airspeed Correction Table in Section V.

BEFORE ENTERING THE AIRPLANE.

(1) Make an exterior inspection in accordance with figure 1-1.

BEFORE STARTING THE ENGINE.

(1) Seats and Seat Belts -- Adjust and lock.
(2) Brakes -- Test and set.
(3) Master Switch -- "ON."
(4) Fuel Valve Handle -- "ON."

STARTING THE ENGINE.

    (1) Carburetor Heat -- Cold.
    (2) Mixture -- Rich.
    (3) Primer -- As required.
    (4) Ignition Switch -- "BOTH."
    (5) Throttle -- Open 1/4".
    (6) Propeller Area -- Clear.
    (7) Starter Handle -- Pull.

BEFORE TAKE-OFF.

    (1) Throttle Setting -- 1700 RPM.
    (2) Engine Instruments -- Within green arc and generator light out.
    (3) Magnetos -- Check (75 RPM maximum differential between magnetos).
    (4) Carburetor Heat -- Check operation.
    (5) Suction Gage -- Check (4. 6 to 5. 4 inches of mercury).
    (6) Flight Controls -- Check.
    (7) Trim Tab -- "TAKE-OFF" setting.
    (8) Cabin Doors -- Latched.
    (9) Flight Instruments and Radios -- Set.

TAKE-OFF.

NORMAL TAKE-OFF.

    (1) Wing Flaps -- Up.
    (2) Carburetor Heat -- Cold.
    (3) Throttle -- Full "OPEN."
    (4) Elevator Control -- Lift nose wheel at 50 MPH.
    (5) Climb Speed -- 72 MPH until all obstacles are cleared, then set up climb speed as shown in "NORMAL CLIMB" paragraph.

MAXIMUM PERFORMANCE TAKE-OFF.

    (1) Wing Flaps -- Up.
    (2) Carburetor Heat -- Cold.
    (3) Brakes -- Hold.
    (4) Throttle -- Full "OPEN."

(5) Brakes -- Release.
(6) Elevator Control -- Slightly tail low.
(7) Climb Speed -- 52 MPH (with obstacles ahead).

CLIMB.

NORMAL CLIMB.

(1) Air Speed -- 75 to 80 MPH.
(2) Power -- Full throttle.
(3) Mixture -- Rich (unless engine is rough).

MAXIMUM PERFORMANCE CLIMB.

(1) Air Speed -- 72 MPH.
(2) Power -- Full throttle.
(3) Mixture -- Rich (unless engine is rough).

CRUISING.

(1) Power -- 2000 to 2750 RPM.
(2) Elevator Trim -- Adjust.
(3) Mixture -- Lean to maximum RPM.

BEFORE LANDING.

(1) Mixture -- Rich.
(2) Carburetor Heat -- Apply full heat before closing throttle.
(3) Airspeed -- 65 to 75 MPH.
(4) Wing Flaps -- As desired below 100 MPH
(5) Airspeed -- 60 to 70 MPH (flaps extended).

NORMAL LANDING.

(1) Touch Down -- Main wheels first.
(2) Landing Roll -- Lower nose wheel gently.
(3) Braking -- Minimum required.

AFTER LANDING.

    (1) Wing Flaps -- Up.
    (2) Carburetor Heat -- Cold.

SECURE AIRCRAFT.

    (1) Mixture -- Idle cut-off.
    (2) All Switches -- Off.
    (3) Parking Brake -- Set.
    (4) Control Lock -- Installed.

DESCRIPTION AND OPERATING DETAILS

The following paragraphs describe the systems and equipment whose function and operation is not obvious when sitting in the airplane. This section also covers in somewhat greater detail some of the items listed in Check List form in Section I that require further explanation.

FUEL SYSTEM.

Fuel is supplied to the engine from two tanks, one in each wing. From these tanks, fuel flows by gravity through a fuel shutoff valve and fuel strainer to the carburetor.

Refer to figure 2-1 for fuel quantity data. For fuel system service information, refer to Lubrication and Servicing Procedures in Section IV.

FUEL STRAINER DRAIN KNOB.

Refer to fuel strainer servicing procedure, Section IV.

FUEL QUANTITY DATA (U.S. GALLONS)

TANKS	USABLE FUEL ALL FLIGHT CONDITIONS	UNUSABLE FUEL	TOTAL FUEL VOLUME
TWO, STANDARD WING (13 GAL. EACH)	22.5	3.5	26.0
TWO, LONG RANGE WING (19 GAL. EACH)	35.0	3.0	38.0

Figure 2-1.

LEFT FUEL TANK
RIGHT FUEL TANK
FUEL
22.5 GALS
ON
OFF
FUEL SHUTOFF
VALVE
FUEL
STRAINER
TO INTAKE
MANIFOLD
ENGINE
PRIMER
THROTTLE
FUEL
SYSTEM
···· SCHEMATIC ····
CARBURETOR
TO ENGINE
CYLINDERS
MIXTURE
CONTROL
KNOB

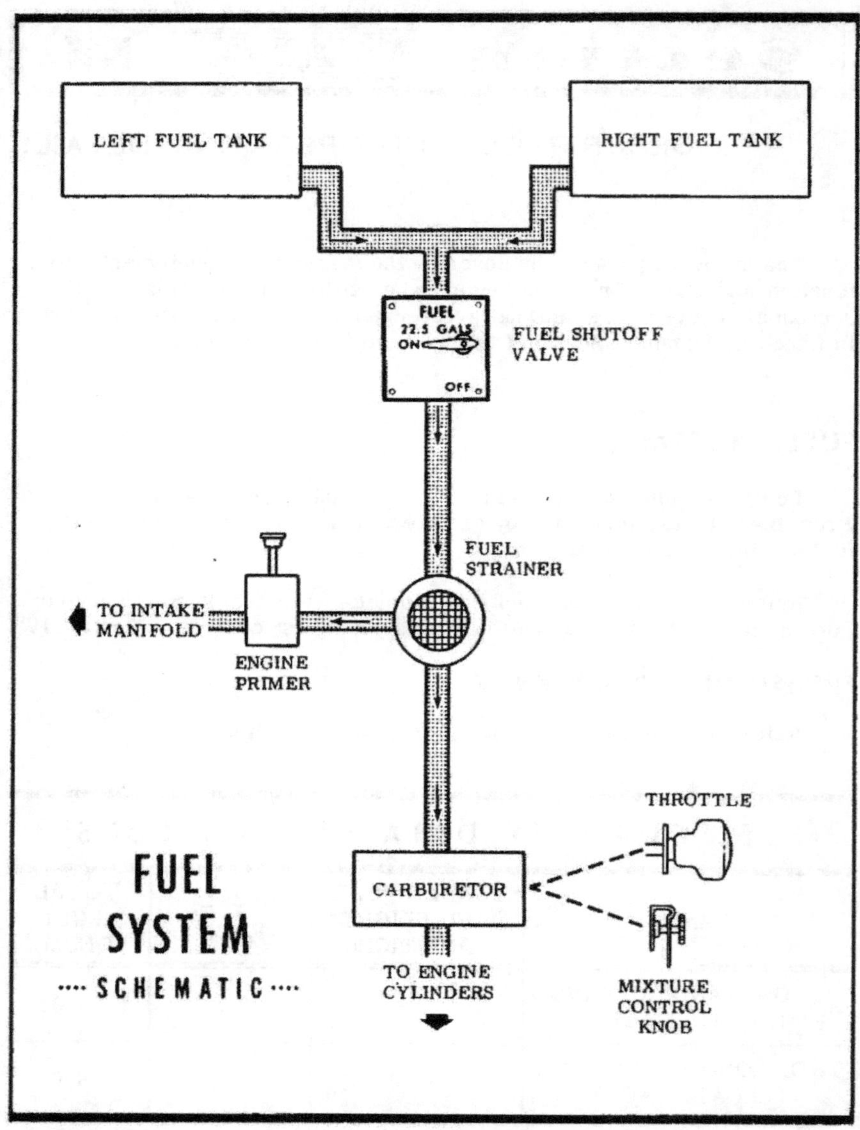

Figure 2-2.

ELECTRICAL SYSTEM.

Electrical energy is supplied by a 14-volt, direct-current system powered by an engine-driven generator. A 12-volt storage battery is located on the right, forward side of the firewall just inside the cowl access door. The master switch controls all electrical circuits except the clock and the ignition system.

FUSES AND CIRCUIT BREAKERS.

Fuses on the instrument panel protect most of the electrical circuits in your airplane. (The clock fuse is located adjacent to the battery.) The circuits controlled by each fuse are indicated above each fuse retainer. Fuse capacity is indicated on each fuse retainer cap. Fuses are removed by pressing the fuse retainers inward and rotating them counterclockwise until they disengage. The faulty fuse may then be lifted out and replaced. Spare fuses are held in a clip on the inside of the map compartment door.

Circuit breaker switches on the instrument panel control and protect the optional rotating beacon and pitot heater circuits.

GENERATOR WARNING LIGHT.

A red generator warning light labeled "GEN," gives an indication of generator output. It will remain off at all times when the generator is functioning properly. The light will not show drainage on the battery. It will illuminate when the battery or external power is turned on prior to starting the engine, and when there is insufficient engine RPM to produce generator current. Also, it will illuminate if generator becomes defective.

LANDING LIGHTS (OPT).

A three-position, push-pull type switch controls the optional landing lights mounted in the leading edge of the left wing. To turn one lamp on for taxiing, pull the switch out to the first stop. To turn both lamps on for landing, pull the switch out to the second stop.

ROTATING BEACON (OPT).

The rotating beacon should not be used when flying through clouds or overcast; the moving beams reflected from water droplets or particles in the atmosphere, particularly at night, can produce vertigo and loss of orientation.

CABIN HEATING AND VENTILATING SYSTEM.

For heated ventilation air, pull the cabin heat knob out the desired amount. Additional ventilating air is provided by pulling out the ventilators located in the upper corners of the windshield.

PARKING BRAKE SYSTEM.

To set parking brake, pull out on the parking brake knob, apply and release toe pressure to the pedals, and then release the parking brake knob. To release the parking brake, apply and release toe pressure on the pedals while checking to see that the parking brake knob is full in.

STARTING ENGINE.

Ordinarily the engine starts easily with one or two strokes of primer in warm temperatures to six strokes in cold weather, with the throttle open approximately 1/4 inch. In extremely cold temperatures, it may be necessary to continue priming while cranking.

Weak intermittent explosions followed by puffs of black smoke from the exhaust stack indicates overpriming or flooding. Excess fuel can be cleared from the combustion chambers by the following procedure: Set the mixture control in full lean position, throttle full open, and crank the engine through several revolutions with the starter. Repeat the starting procedure without any additional priming.

If the engine is underprimed (most likely in cold weather with a cold engine) it will not fire at all, and additional priming will be necessary. As soon as the cylinders begin to fire, open the throttle slightly to keep it running.

After starting, if the oil gage does not begin to show pressure within 30 seconds in the summertime and about twice that long in very cold weather, stop engine and investigate. Lack of oil pressure can cause serious engine damage. After starting, avoid the use of carburetor heat unless icing conditions prevail.

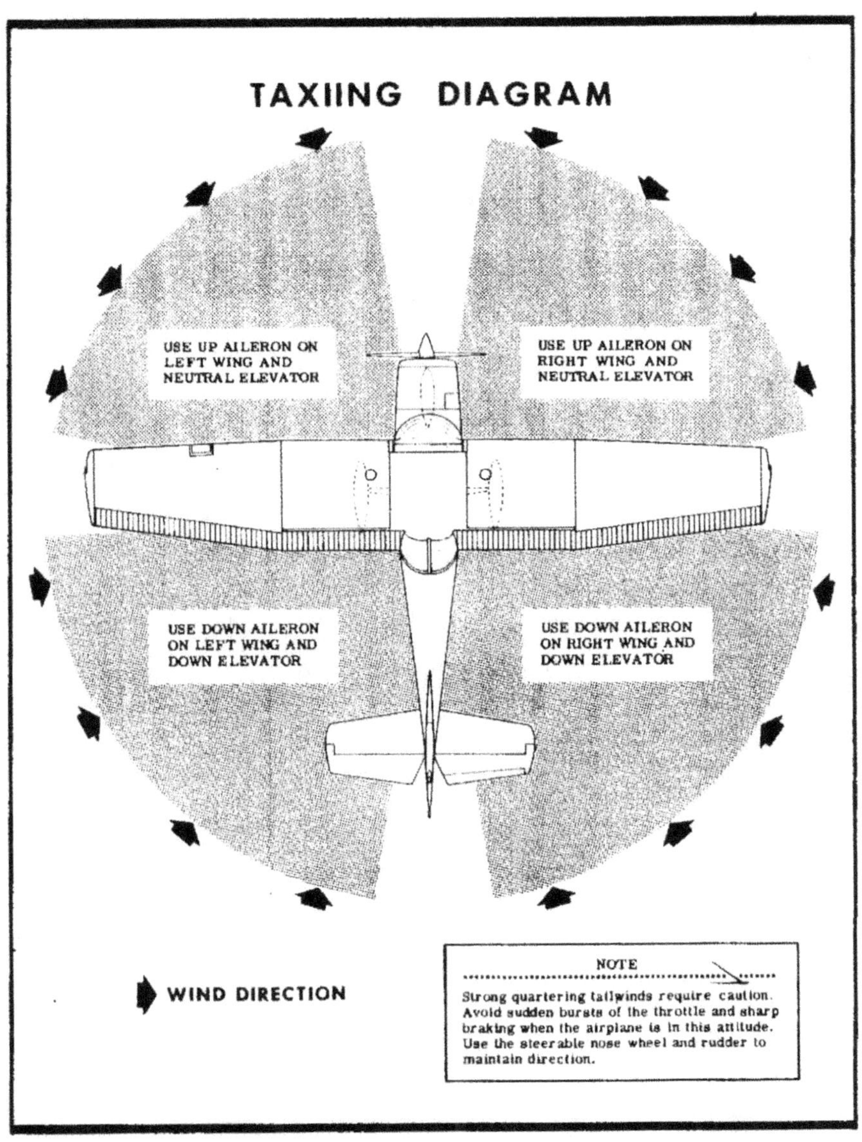

TAXIING DIAGRAM
USE UP AILERON ON LEFT WING AND NEUTRAL ELEVATOR
USE UP AILERON ON RIGHT WING AND NEUTRAL ELEVATOR
USE DOWN AILERON ON LEFT WING AND DOWN ELEVATOR
USE DOWN AILERON ON RIGHT WING AND DOWN ELEVATOR
WIND DIRECTION
NOTE
Strong quartering tailwinds require caution. Avoid sudden bursts of the throttle and sharp braking when the airplane is in this attitude. Use the steerable nose wheel and rudder to maintain direction.

Figure 2-3.

TAXIING.

When taxiing, it is important that speed and use of brakes be held to a minimum and that all controls be utilized (see taxiing diagram, figure 2-3) to maintain directional control and balance.

Taxiing over loose gravel or cinders should be done at low engine speed to avoid abrasion and stone damage to the propeller tips.

BEFORE TAKE-OFF.

WARM-UP.

Most of the warm-up will have been conducted during taxi, and additional warm-up before take-off should be restricted to the checks outlined in Section I.   Since the engine is closely cowled for efficient in-flight cooling, precautions should be taken to avoid overheating on the ground.

MAGNETO CHECK.

The magneto check should be made at 1700 RPM as follows: Move the ignition switch first to "R" position and note RPM.   Then move switch back to "BOTH" position to clear the other set of plugs.   Then move switch to "L" position and note RPM.   The difference between the two magnetos operated individually should not be more than 75 RPM.   If there is a doubt concerning the operation of the ignition system, RPM checks at higher engine speeds will usually confirm whether a deficiency exists.

An absence of RPM drop may be an indication of faulty grounding of one side of the ignition system or should be cause for suspicion that the magneto has been "bumped-up" and is set in advance of the setting specified.

TAKE-OFF.

POWER CHECKS.

It is important to check full-throttle engine operation early in the take-off run.   Any signs of rough engine operation or sluggish engine acceleration is good cause for discontinuing the take-off.   If this occurs, you are

justified in making a thorough full-throttle, static runup before another
take-off is attempted. The engine should run smoothly and turn approximately 2375 to 2475 RPM with carburetor heat off.

Full throttle runups over loose gravel are especially harmful to propeller tips. When take-offs must be made over a gravel surface, it is
very important that the throttle be advanced slowly. This allows the airplane to start rolling before high RPM is developed, and the gravel will
be blown back of the propeller rather than pulled into it. When unavoid-
able small dents appear in the propeller blades, they should be immediately corrected as described in Section IV.

Prior to take-off from fields above 5000 feet elevation, the mixture
should be leaned to give maximum RPM in a full-throttle, static runup.

FLAP SETTINGS.

Normal and obstacle clearance take-offs are performed with flaps up.
The use of 10° flaps will shorten the ground run approximately 10%, but
this advantage is lost in the climb to a 50-foot obstacle. Therefore the
use of 10° flap is reserved for minimum ground runs or for take-off
from soft or rough fields with no obstacles ahead.

If 10° of flaps are used in ground runs, it is preferable to leave them
extended rather than retract them in the climb to the obstacle. The ex-
ception to this rule would be in a high altitude take-off in hot weather
where climb would be marginal with flaps 10°.

Flap deflections of 30° and 40° are not recommended at any time for
take-off.

PERFORMANCE CHARTS.

Consult the take-off chart in Section V for take-off distances under
various gross weight, altitude, and headwind conditions.

CROSSWIND TAKE-OFFS.

Take-offs into strong crosswinds normally are performed with the
minimum flap setting necessary for the field length, to minimize the
drift angle immediately after take-off. The airplane is accelerated to
a speed slightly higher than normal, then pulled off abruptly to prevent
possible settling back to the runway while drifting. When clear of the
ground, make a coordinated turn into the wind to correct for drift.

CLIMB.

CLIMB DATA.

For detailed data, see Maximum Rate-of-Climb Data chart in Section V.

CLIMB SPEEDS.

Normal climbs are conducted at 75 to 80 MPH with flaps up and full throttle, for best engine cooling. The mixture should be full rich unless the engine is rough due to too rich a mixture. The best rate-of-climb speeds range from 72 MPH at sea level to 66 MPH at 10,000 feet. If an obstruction dictates the use of a steep climb angle, the best angle-of-climb speed should be used with flaps up and full throttle. These speeds vary from 52 MPH at sea level to 60 MPH at 10,000 feet.

NOTE

Steep climbs at these low speeds should be of short duration to allow improved engine cooling.

GO-AROUND CLIMB.

In a balked landing (go-around) climb, the wing flap setting should be reduced to 20° immediately after full power is applied. Upon reaching a safe airspeed, the flaps should be slowly retracted to the full up position.

CRUISE.

Normal cruising is done at 65% to 75% of METO power. The settings required to obtain these powers at various altitudes and outside air temperatures can be determined by using your Cessna Power Computer or the OPERATIONAL DATA, Section V.

Cruising can be done most efficiently at high altitude because of the higher true airspeeds obtainable at the same power. This is illustrated in the following table for 70% power.

<table>
<tr><th colspan="3">OPTIMUM CRUISE PERFORMANCE</th></tr>
<tr><th>ALTITUDE</th><th>RPM</th><th>TRUE AIRSPEED</th></tr>
<tr><td>Sea Level</td><td>* 2430</td><td>111</td></tr>
<tr><td>5000 feet</td><td>* 2550</td><td>116</td></tr>
<tr><td>9000 feet</td><td>* Full Throttle</td><td>120</td></tr>
<tr><td></td><td colspan="2">* 70% POWER</td></tr>
</table>

STALLS.

The stall characteristics are conventional for the flaps up and flaps down condition. Slight elevator buffeting may occur just before the stall with flaps down.

The stalling speeds are shown in Section V for aft c.g., full gross weight conditions. They are presented as calibrated airspeeds because indicated airspeeds are unreliable near the stall. Other loadings result in slower stalling speeds. The stall warning horn produces a steady signal 5 to 10 MPH before the actual stall is reached and remains on until the airplane flight attitude is changed.

LANDING.

Normal landings are made power off with any flap setting. Approach glides are normally made at 65 to 75 MPH with flaps up, or 60 to 70 MPH with flaps down, depending upon the turbulence of the air.

SHORT FIELD LANDINGS.

For a short field landing, make a power off approach at 58 MPH with flaps 40° and land on the main wheels first. Immediately after touchdown, lower the nose gear to the ground and apply heavy braking as required. · Raising the flaps after landing will provide more efficient braking.

CROSSWIND LANDINGS.

When landing in a strong crosswind, use the minimum flap setting required for the field length. Use a wing low, crab, or a combination method of drift correction and land in a nearly level attitude. Hold a straight course with the steerable nosewheel and occasional braking if necessary.

COLD WEATHER OPERATION.

Prior to starting on cold mornings, it is advisable to pull the propeller through several times by hand to "break loose" or "limber" the oil, thus conserving battery energy. In extremely cold (0°F and lower) weather the use of an external preheater is recommended whenever possible to reduce wear and abuse to the engine and the electrical system. Cold weather starting procedures are as follows:

With Preheat:

    (1) Clear propeller.
    (2) Pull master switch "ON."
    (3) With magneto switch "OFF" and throttle closed, prime the engine four to ten strokes as the engine is being turned over.

NOTE

Use heavy strokes of primer for best atomization of fuel. After priming, push primer all the way in and turn to locked position to avoid possibility of engine drawing fuel through the primer.

    (4) Turn magneto switch to "BOTH."
    (5) Open throttle 1/4" and engage starter.

Without Preheat:

    (1) Prime the engine eight to ten heavy strokes while the propeller is being turned by hand.
    (2) Clear propeller.
    (3) Pull master switch "ON."
    (4) Turn magneto switch to "BOTH."
    (5) Open throttle 1/4".
    (6) Pull carburetor air heat knob full on.
    (7) Engage starter and continue to prime engine until it is running smoothly.

(8) Keep carburetor heat on until engine has warmed up.

NOTE

If the engine does not start the first time, it is probable
that the spark plugs have been frosted over. Preheat
must be used before another start is attempted.

During cold weather operations, no indication will be apparent on the
oil temperature gage prior to take-off if outside air temperatures are very
cold. After a suitable warm-up period (2 to 5 minutes at 1000 RPM),
accelerate the engine several times to higher engine RPM. If the engine
accelerates smoothly and the oil pressure remains normal and steady,
the airplane is ready for take-off.

When operating in sub-zero temperature, avoid using partial carburetor heat. Partial heat may increase the carburetor air temperature to
the 32° to 70° range, where icing is critical under certain atmospheric
conditions.

Refer to Section VI for cold weather equipment.

OPERATING LIMITATIONS

OPERATIONS AUTHORIZED.

Your Cessna exceeds the requirements of airworthiness as set forth by the United States Government, and is certificated under FAA Type Certificate No. 3A19 as Cessna Model No. 150F.

With standard equipment, the airplane is approved for day and night operation under VFR. Additional optional equipment is available to increase its utility and to make it authorized for use under IFR day and night.

Your airplane must be operated in accordance with all FAA-approved markings, placards and check lists in the airplane. If there is any information in this section which contradicts the FAA-approved markings, placards and check lists, it is to be disregarded.

MANEUVERS-UTILITY CATEGORY.

This airplane is not designed for purely aerobatic flight. However, in the acquisition of various certificates such as commercial pilot, instrument pilot and flight instructor, certain maneuvers are required by the FAA. All of these maneuvers are permitted in this airplane when operated in the utility category. In connection with the foregoing, the following gross weight and flight load factors apply, with maximum entry speeds for maneuvers as shown:

Gross Weight . . . . 1600 lbs

Flight Maneuvering Load Factor, *Flaps Up . . . +4.4   -1.76

Flight Maneuvering Load Factor, *Flaps Down . . +3.5

*The design load factors are 150% of the above, and in all cases, the structure meets or exceeds design loads.

No acrobatic maneuvers are approved except those listed below:

MANEUVER	RECOMMENDED ENTRY SPEED
Chandelles	109 MPH (95 knots)
Lazy Eights	109 MPH (95 knots)
Steep Turns	109 MPH (95 knots)
Spins	Use Slow Deceleration
Stalls	Use Slow Deceleration

During prolonged spins, the aircraft engine may stop; however, spin recovery is not adversely affected by engine stoppage. Intentional spins with wing flaps extended are prohibited.

Acrobatics that may impose high inverted loads should not be attempted. The important thing to bear in mind in flight maneuvers is that the Cessna 150 is clean in aerodynamic design and will build up speed quickly with the nose down. Proper speed control is an essential requirement for execution of any maneuver, and care should always be exercised to avoid excessive speed which in turn can impose excessive loads. In the execution of all maneuvers, avoid abrupt use of controls.

AIRSPEED LIMITATIONS.

The following are the certificated calibrated airspeed limits for the Cessna 150:

Maximum (Glide or dive, smooth air)	162 MPH (red line)
Caution Range	120-162 MPH (yellow arc)
Normal Range	56-120 MPH (green arc)
Flap Operating Range	49-100 MPH (white arc)
Maneuvering Speed*	109 MPH

   *The maximum speed at which you can use abrupt
    control travel without exceeding the design load
    factor.

ENGINE OPERATION LIMITATIONS.

Power and Speed	100 BHP at 2750 RPM

ENGINE INSTRUMENT MARKINGS.

OIL TEMPERATURE GAGE.
    Normal Operating Range . . . . Green Arc
    Maximum Allowable . . . . 225°F Red Line

OIL PRESSURE GAGE.
    Minimum Idling . . . . 10 PSI (red line)
    Normal Operating Range . . . . 30-60 PSI (green arc)
    . Maximum . . . . 100 PSI (red line)

FUEL QUANTITY INDICATORS.
    Empty (1.75 gallons unusable each tank) . . . . E (red line)

TACHOMETER.
    Normal Operating Range:
        At sea level . . . . 2000-2550 (inner green arc)
        At 5000 feet . . . . .2000-2650 (middle green arc)
        At 10,000 feet . . . . 2000-2750 (outer green arc)
    Maximum Allowable . . . . 2750 (red line)

WEIGHT AND BALANCE.

The following information will enable you to operate your Cessna
within the prescribed weight and center of gravity limitations. To figure
the weight and balance for your particular airplane, use the Sample Prob-
lem, Loading Graph, and Center of Gravity Moment Envelope as follows:

Take the licensed Empty Weight and Moment/1000 from the Weight
and Balance Data sheet, plus any changes noted on forms FAA-337,
carried in your airplane, and write them down in the proper columns.
Using the Loading Graph, determine the moment/1000 of each item to be
carried. Total the weights and moments/1000 and use the Center of
Gravity Moment Envelope to determine whether the point falls within the
envelope, and if the loading is acceptable.

SAMPLE LOADING PROBLEM	Sample Airplane			Your Airplane	
	Weight (lbs)	Moment (lb-ins. /1000)		Weight	Moment
1. Licensed Empty Weight (Sample Airplane)	1038	34.2			
2. Oil - 6Qts.*	11	-0.1		11	-0.1
3. Pilot & Passenger	340	13.3			
4. Fuel - Std. Tanks (22.5 Gal at 6#/Gal)	135	5.7			
5. Baggage-Area 1 (or children on child's seat)	76	4.9			
6. Baggage-Area 2	0	0.0			
7. Total Aircraft Weight (Loaded)	1600	58.0			

8. Locate this point (1600 at 58.0) on the center of gravity envelope and since this point falls within envelope the loading is acceptable.

*Note; Normally full oil may be assumed for all flights.

BAGGAGE LOADING AND TIE-DOWN

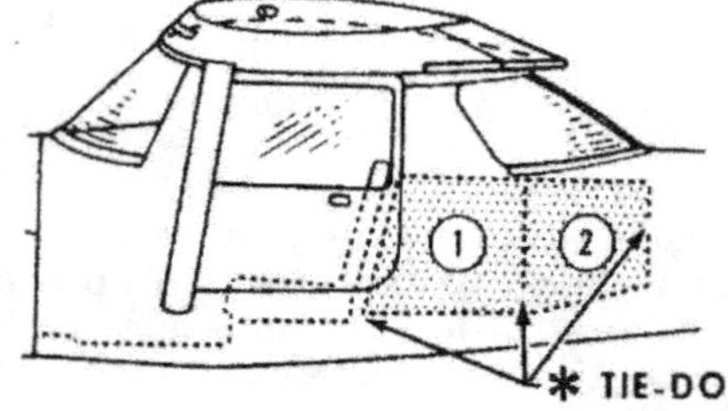

BAGGAGE AREA
MAXIMUM ALLOWABLE LOADS

AREA ① = 120 POUNDS
AREA ② = 40 POUNDS
AREAS ① + ② = 120 POUNDS

* A cargo tie-down net is provided to secure baggage in the baggage area. The net attaches to six tie-down rings. Two rings are located on the floor just aft of the seat backs and one ring is located two inches above the floor on each cabin wall at the aft end of area ①. Two additional rings are located at the top, aft end of area ②. At least four rings should be used to restrain the maximum baggage load of 120#.

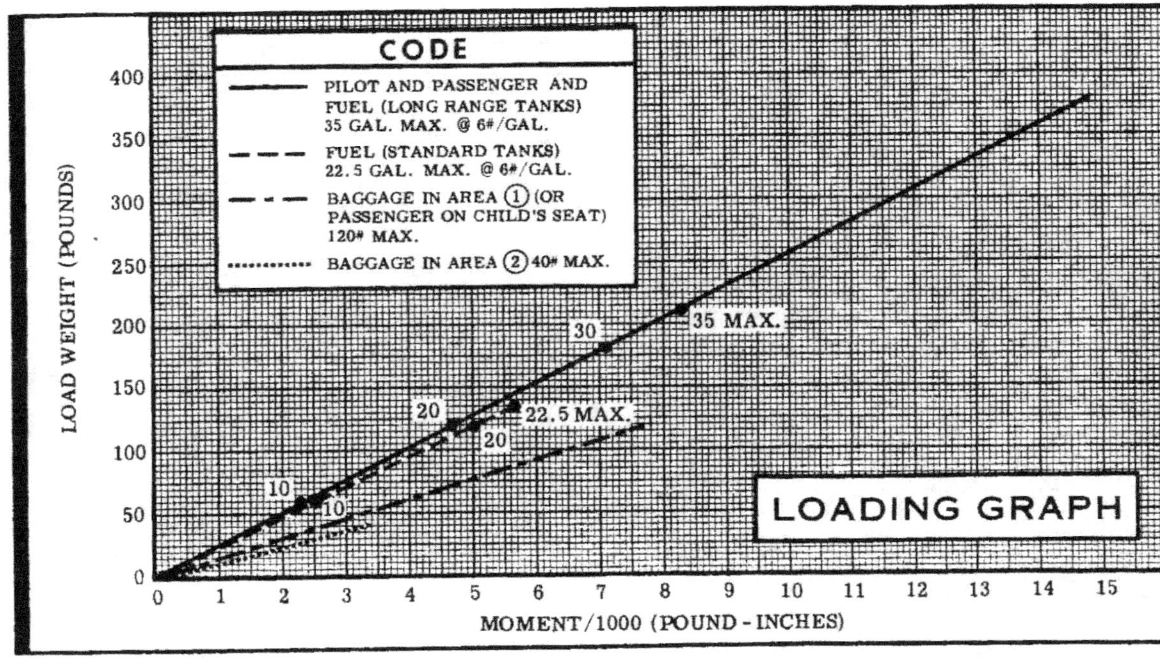

CODE
PILOT AND PASSENGER AND FUEL (LONG RANGE TANKS) 35 GAL. MAX. @ 6#/GAL.
FUEL (STANDARD TANKS) 22.5 GAL. MAX. @ 6#/GAL.
BAGGAGE IN AREA 1 (OR PASSENGER ON CHILD'S SEAT) 120# MAX.
BAGGAGE IN AREA 2 40# MAX.
35 MAX.
30
20
22.5 MAX.
20
10
10
400
350
300
250
200
150
100
50
0
LOAD WEIGHT (POUNDS)
0 1 2 3 4 5 6 7 8 9 10 11 12 13 14 15
MOMENT/1000 (POUND - INCHES)
LOADING GRAPH

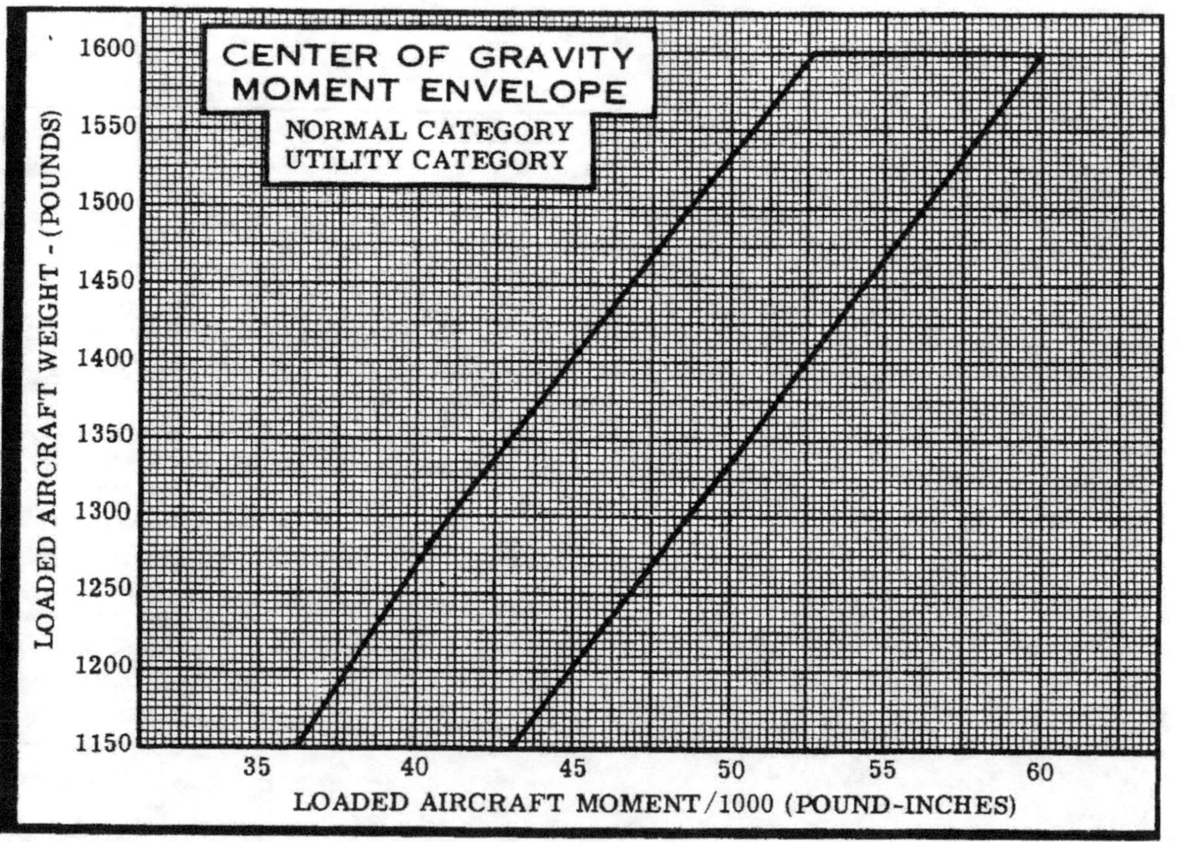

CENTER OF GRAVITY
MOMENT ENVELOPE
NORMAL CATEGORY
UTILITY CATEGORY
LOADED AIRCRAFT WEIGHT - (POUNDS)
1600
1550
1500
1450
1400
1350
1300
1250
1200
1150
LOADED AIRCRAFT MOMENT/1000 (POUND-INCHES)
35
40
45
50
55
60

CARE OF THE AIRPLANE

If your airplane is to retain that new-plane performance, stamina, and dependability, certain inspection and maintenance requirements must be followed. It is always wise to follow a planned schedule of lubrication and maintenance based on the climatic and flying conditions encountered in your locality.

Keep in touch with your Cessna dealer, and take advantage of his knowledge and experience. He knows your airplane and how to maintain it. He will remind you when lubrications and oil changes are necessary and about other seasonal and periodic services.

GROUND HANDLING.

The airplane is most easily and safely maneuvered by hand with a tow-bar attached to the nose wheel.

NOTE

When using the tow-bar, never exceed the turning angle of 30°, either side of center, or damage to the gear will result.

MOORING YOUR AIRPLANE.

Proper tie-down is the best precaution against damage to your parked airplane by gusty or strong winds.

To tie down your airplane securely, proceed as follows:

(1) Set parking brake and install control wheel lock.
(2) Install a surface control lock between each aileron and flap.
(3) Tie sufficiently strong ropes or chains (700 pounds tensile strength) to wing and tail tie-down fittings, and secure each rope

to ramp tie-down.

(4) Install a surface control lock over the fin and rudder.

(5) Install a pitot tube cover.

(6) Tie a rope to an exposed portion of the engine mount and secure the opposite end to a ramp tie-down.

WINDSHIELD-WINDOWS.

The plastic windshield and windows should be kept clean and waxed at all times. To prevent scratches and crazing, wash them carefully with plenty of soap and water, using the palm of the hand to feel and dislodge dirt and mud. A soft cloth, chamois or sponge may be used, but only to carry water to the surface. Rinse thoroughly, then dry with a clean, moist chamois. Rubbing the surface of the plastic with a dry cloth builds up an electrostatic charge so that it attracts dust particles in the air. Wiping with a moist chamois will remove both the dust and this charge.

Remove oil and grease with a cloth moistened with kerosene. Never use gasoline, benzine, alcohol, acetone, carbon tetrachloride, fire extinguisher or anti-ice fluid, lacquer thinner or glass cleaner. These materials will soften the plastic and may cause it to craze.

After removing dirt and grease, if the surface is not badly scratched, it should be waxed with a good grade of commercial wax. The wax will fill in minor scratches and help prevent further scratching. Apply a thin, even coat of wax and bring it to a high polish by rubbing lightly with a clean, dry, soft flannel cloth. Do not use a power buffer; the heat generated by the buffing pad may soften the plastic.

Do not use a canvas cover on the windshield unless freezing rain or sleet is anticipated. Canvas covers may scratch the plastic surface.

PAINTED SURFACES.

The painted exterior surfaces of your new Cessna require an initial curing period which may be as long as 90 days after the finish is applied. During this curing period some precautions should be taken to avoid damaging the finish or interfering with the curing process. The finish should be cleaned only by washing with clean water and mild soap, followed by a rinse with water and drying with cloths or a chamois. Do not use polish or wax, which would exclude air from the surface, during this 90-day curing period. Do not rub or buff the finish and avoid flying through rain, hail or sleet.

Once the finish has cured completely, it may be waxed with a good automotive wax. A heavier coating of wax on the leading edges of the wings and tail and on the engine nose cap and propeller spinner will help reduce the abrasion encountered in these areas.

ALUMINUM SURFACES.

The clad aluminum surfaces of your Cessna require only a minimum of care to keep them bright and clean. The airplane may be washed with clear water to remove dirt; oil and grease may be removed with gasoline, naphtha, carbon tetrachloride or other non-alkaline solvents. Dulled aluminum surfaces may be cleaned effectively with an aircraft aluminum polish.

After cleaning, and periodically thereafter, waxing with a good automotive wax will preserve the bright appearance and retard corrosion. Regular waxing is especially recommended for airplanes operated in salt water areas as a protection against corrosion.

PROPELLER CARE.

Preflight inspection of propeller blades for nicks, and wiping them occasionally with an oily cloth to clean off grass and bug stains will assure long, trouble-free service. It is vital that small nicks on the propellers, particularly near the tips and on the leading edges, are dressed out as soon as possible since these nicks produce stress concentrations, and if ignored, may result in cracks. Never use an alkaline cleaner on the blades; remove grease and dirt with carbon tetrachloride or Stoddard solvent.

INTERIOR CARE.

To remove dust and loose dirt from the upholstery, headliner, and carpet, clean the interior regularly with a vacuum cleaner.

Blot up any spilled liquid promptly, with cleansing tissue or rags. Don't pat the spot; press the blotting material firmly and hold it for several seconds. Continue blotting until no more liquid is taken up. Scrape off sticky materials with a dull knife, then spot-clean the area.

Oily spots may be cleaned with household spot removers, used sparingly. Before using any solvent, read the instructions on the container and test it on an obscure place on the fabric to be cleaned. Never saturate the fabric with a volatile solvent; it may damage the padding and backing materials.

Soiled upholstery and carpet may be cleaned with foam-type detergent, used according to the manufacturer's instructions. To minimize wetting the fabric, keep the foam as dry as possible and remove it with a vacuum cleaner.

The plastic trim, instrument panel and control knobs need only be wiped off with a damp cloth. Oil and grease on the control wheel and control knobs can be removed with a cloth moistened with kerosene. Volatile solvents, such as mentioned in paragraphs on care of the windshield, must never be used since they soften and craze the plastic.

INSPECTION SERVICE AND INSPECTION PERIODS.

With your airplane you will receive an Owner's Service Policy. Coupons attached to the policy entitle you to an initial inspection and the first 100-hour inspection at no charge. If you take delivery from your Dealer, he will perform the initial inspection before delivery of the airplane to you. If you pick up the airplane at the factory, plan to take it to your Dealer reasonably soon after you take delivery on it. This will permit him to check it over and to make any minor adjustments that may appear necessary. Also, plan an inspection by your Dealer at 100 hours or 180 days, whichever comes first. This inspection also is performed by your Dealer for you at no charge. While these important inspections will be performed for you by any Cessna Dealer, in most cases you will prefer to have the Dealer from whom you purchased the airplane accomplish this work.

Federal Aviation Regulations require that all airplanes have a periodic (annual) inspection as prescribed by the administrator, and performed by a person designated by the administrator. In addition, 100-hour periodic inspections made by an "appropriately-rated mechanic" are required if the airplane is flown for hire. The Cessna Aircraft Company recommends the 100-hour periodic inspection for your airplane. The procedure for this 100-hour inspection has been carefully worked out by the factory and is followed by the Cessna Dealer Organization. The complete familiarity of the Cessna Dealer Organization with Cessna equipment and with factory-approved procedures provides the highest type of service possible at lower cost.

AIRPLANE FILE.

There are miscellaneous data, information and licenses that are a part of the airplane file. The following is a check list for that file. In addition, a periodic check should be made of the latest Federal Aviation Regulations to insure that all data requirements are met.

A. To be displayed in the airplane at all times:

   (1) Aircraft Airworthiness Certificate (Form FAA-1362).
 · (2) Aircraft Registration Certificate (Form FAA-500A).
   (3) Airplane Radio Station License (Form FCC-404, if transmitter installed).

B. To be carried in the airplane at all times:

   (1) Weight and Balance, and associated papers (latest copy of the Repair and Alteration Form, Form FAA-337, if applicable).
   (2) Airplane Equipment List.

C. To be made available upon request:

   (1) Airplane Log Book.
   (2) Engine Log Book.

NOTE

Cessna recommends that these items, plus the Owner's Manual and the "Cessna Flight Guide" (Flight Computer), be carried in the airplane at all times.

Most of the items listed are required by the United States Federal Aviation Regulations. Since the regulations of other nations may require other documents and data, owners of exported airplanes should check with their own aviation officials to determine their individual requirements.

LUBRICATION AND SERVICING PROCEDURES

Specific servicing information is provided here for items requiring daily attention. A Servicing Intervals Check List is included to inform the pilot when to have other items checked and serviced.

DAILY

FUEL TANK FILLERS:
>   Service after each flight with 80/87 minimum grade fuel. The capacity of each wing tank is 13 gallons for standard fuel tanks, 19 gallons for optional long range tanks.

FUEL STRAINER:
>   On the first flight of the day and after each refueling, pull out fuel strainer drain knob (located just inside cowl access door) for about four seconds, to clear fuel strainer of possible water and sediment. Release drain knob, then check that strainer drain is closed after draining.

OIL FILLER:
>   When preflight check shows low oil level, service with aviation grade engine oil; SAE 20 below 40°F. and SAE 40 above 40°F. Your Cessna was delivered from the factory with straight mineral oil (non-detergent) and should be operated with straight mineral oil for the first 25 hours. The use of mineral oil during the 25-hour break-in period will help seat the piston rings and will result in less oil consumption. After the first 25 hours, either mineral oil or detergent oil may be used. If a detergent oil is used, it must conform to Continental Motors Corporation Specification MHS-24. Your Cessna Dealer can supply an approved brand.

OIL DIPSTICK:
>   Check oil level before each flight. Do not operate on less than 4 quarts. To minimize loss of oil through breather, fill to 5 quart level for normal flights of less than 3 hours. For extended flight, fill to 6 quarts. If optional oil filter is installed, one additional quart is required when the filter element is changed.

SERVICING INTERVALS CHECK LIST

EACH 50 HOURS

BATTERY -- Check and service. Check oftener (at least every 30 days) if operating in hot weather.

ENGINE OIL AND OIL FILTER -- Change engine oil and replace filter element. If optional oil filter is not installed, change oil and clean screen every 25 hours. Change engine oil at least every four months even though less than 50 hours have been accumulated. Reduce periods for prolonged operation in dusty areas, cold climates, or when short flights and long idle periods result in sludging conditions.

CARBURETOR AIR FILTER -- Clean or replace. Under extremely dusty conditions, daily maintenance of the filter is recommended.

NOSE GEAR TORQUE LINKS -- Lubricate.

EACH 100 HOURS

BRAKE MASTER CYLINDERS -- Check and fill.

SHIMMY DAMPENER -- Check and fill

FUEL STRAINER -- Disassemble and clean.

FUEL TANK SUMP DRAINS -- Drain water and sediment.

FUEL LINE DRAIN PLUG -- Drain water and sediment.

VACUUM SYSTEM OIL SEPARATOR (OPT) -- Clean.

SUCTION RELIEF VALVE INLET SCREEN (OPT) -- Clean.

EACH 500 HOURS

VACUUM SYSTEM AIR FILTER (OPT) -- Replace filter element. Replace sooner if suction gage reading drops to 4. 6 in. Hg.

WHEEL BEARINGS -- Lubricate. Lubricate at first 100 hours and at 500 hours thereafter.

AS REQUIRED

NOSE GEAR SHOCK STRUT -- Keep inflated and filled.

GYRO INSTRUMENT AIR FILTERS (OPT) -- Replace at instrument overhaul.

OWNER FOLLOW-UP SYSTEM ———

Your Cessna Dealer has an owner follow-up system to notify you when he receives information that applies to your Cessna. In addition, if you wish, you may choose to receive similar notification directly from the Cessna Service Department. A subscription card is supplied in your airplane file for your use, should you choose to request this service. Your Cessna Dealer will be glad to supply you with details concerning these follow-up programs, and stands ready through his Service Department to supply you with fast, efficient, low cost service.

Section V

OPERATIONAL DATA

The operational data shown on the following pages are compiled from actual tests with airplane and engine in good condition, and using average piloting technique and best power mixture. You will find this data a valuable aid when planning your flights. However, inasmuch as the number of variables included precludes great accuracy, an ample fuel reserve should be provided. The range performance shown makes no allowance for wind, navigational error, pilot technique, warm-up, take-off, climb etc. which may be different on each flight you make. All of these factors must be considered when estimating reserve fuel.

To realize the maximum usefulness from your Cessna, you should take advantage of its high cruising speeds. However, if range is of primary importance, it may pay you to fly at a low cruising RPM, thereby increasing your range and allowing you to make the trip non-stop with ample fuel reserve. The range table on page 5-4 should be used to solve flight planning problems of this nature.

In the table (figure 5-4), range and endurance are given for lean mixture from 2500 feet to 12,500 feet. All figures are based on zero wind, 22.5 and 35.0 gallons of fuel for cruise, McCauley 1A100/MCM6950 propeller, 1600 pounds gross weight, and standard atmospheric conditions. Mixture is leaned to maximum RPM. Allowances for fuel reserve, headwinds, take-offs and climb, and variations in mixture leaning technique should be made as no allowances are shown on the chart. Other indeterminate variables such as carburetor metering characteristics, engine and propeller conditions, and turbulence of the atmosphere may account for variations of 10% or more in maximum range.

Remember that the charts contained herein are based on standard day conditions. For more precise power, fuel consumption, and endurance information, consult the Cessna Flight Guide (Power Computer) supplied with your aircraft. With the Flight Guide, you can easily take into account temperature variations from standard at any flight altitude.

AIRSPEED CORRECTION TABLE

(Flaps Up)

IAS	40	50	60	70	80	90	100	110	120	130	140
CAS	51	57	65	73	82	91	100	109	118	127	136

(Flaps Down)

IAS	40	50	60	70	80	90	100				
CAS	49	55	63	72	81	89	98				

Figure 5-1.

STALLING SPEEDS

=Power Off=   MPH = CAS

Gross Weight 1600 lbs. CONDITION	ANGLE OF BANK			
	0°	20°	40°	60°
Flaps UP	55	57	63	78
Flaps 20°	49	51	56	70
Flaps 40°	48	49	54	67

Figure 5-2.

—TAKE-OFF DISTANCE—

FLAPS RETRACTED ....
HARD SURFACE RUNWAY ....

GROSS WT. LBS.	IAS 50 FT. MPH	HEAD WIND KNOTS	AT SEA LEVEL & 59° F.		AT 2500 FT. & 50° F.		AT 5000 FT. & 41° F.		AT 7500 FT. & 32° F.	
			GROUND RUN	TOTAL TO CLEAR 50 FT. OBS	GROUND RUN	TOTAL TO CLEAR 50 FT. OBS	GROUND RUN	TOTAL TO CLEAR 50 FT. OBS	GROUND RUN	TOTAL TO CLEAR 50 FT. OBS
1600	64	0	735	1385	910	1660	1115	1985	1360	2440
		10	500	1035	630	1250	780	1510	970	1875
		20	305	730	395	890	505	1090	640	1375

NOTE: Increase the distances 10% for each 35° F. increase in temperature above standard for the particular altitude.

—MAXIMUM RATE-OF-CLIMB DATA—

GROSS WEIGHT LBS.	AT SEA LEVEL & 59° F.			AT 5000 FT. & 41° F.			AT 10000 FT. & 23° F.			
	IAS, MPH	RATE OF CLIMB FT./MIN.	FUEL USED. GAL.	IAS, MPH	RATE OF CLIMB FT./MIN.	FUEL USED FROM S.L., GAL.	IAS, MPH	RATE OF CLIMB FT./MIN.	FUEL USED FROM S.L., GAL.	
1600	72	670	.6	69	440	1.6	66	220	3.0	

NOTE: Flaps retracted, full throttle, mixture leaned to smooth operation above 5000 ft. Fuel used includes warm-up and take-off allowances.

—LANDING DISTANCE—

FLAPS LOWERED TO 40° - POWER OFF
HARD SURFACE RUNWAY - ZERO WIND

GROSS WEIGHT LBS.	APPROACH SPEED, IAS, MPH	AT SEA LEVEL & 59° F.		AT 2500 FT. & 50° F.		AT 5000 FT. & 41° F.		AT 7500 FT. & 32° F.	
		GROUND ROLL	TOTAL TO CLEAR 50 FT. OBS	GROUND ROLL	TOTAL TO CLEAR 50 FT. OBS	GROUND ROLL	TOTAL TO CLEAR 50 FT. OBS	GROUND ROLL	TOTAL TO CLEAR 50 FT. OBS
1600	58	445	1075	470	1135	495	1195	520	1255

NOTE: Decrease the distances shown by 10% for each 4 knots of headwind. Increase the distance by 10% for each 60° F. temperature increase above standard.

Figure 5-3.

| ALTITUDE | RPM | %BHP | TAS-MPH | GAL/HR. | END. HOURS | | RANGE, MILES | |
					STANDARD 22.5 GAL.	LONG RANGE 35 GAL.	STANDARD 22.5 GAL.	LONG RANGE 35 GAL.
2500	2750	94	126	7.2	3.1	4.9	395	610
	2700	89	124	6.8	3.3	5.2	410	640
	2600	79	119	6.0	3.8	5.9	450	700
	2500	71	114	5.3	4.3	6.6	485	755
	2400	63	108	4.7	4.8	7.4	515	805
	2300	56	102	4.2	5.3	8.3	540	845
	2200	50	95	3.8	5.9	9.1	555	865
	2100	45	87	3.5	6.4	10.0	560	870
5000	2750	87	126	6.6	3.4	5.3	430	670
	2700	82	124	6.2	3.6	5.6	450	700
	2600	74	119	5.5	4.1	6.3	485	755
	2500	66	113	4.9	4.6	7.1	515	800
	2400	58	107	4.4	5.1	7.9	545	845
	2300	53	100	4.0	5.6	8.7	555	865
	2200	47	92	3.7	6.1	9.5	560	875
	2100	44	86	3.4	6.6	10.2	565	875
7500	2700	76	123	5.7	3.9	6.1	485	755
	2600	68	117	5.1	4.4	6.8	515	805
	2500	61	111	4.6	4.9	7.6	540	845
	2400	55	104	4.2	5.4	8.3	555	865
	2300	50	97	3.8	5.9	9.1	565	880
	2200	46	90	3.6	6.3	9.7	560	875
	2100	44	85	3.4	6.6	10.2	560	870
10,000	2700	71	122	5.3	4.2	6.6	515	805
	2600	64	116	4.8	4.7	7.3	540	840
	2500	58	109	4.4	5.1	8.0	560	870
	2400	52	101	4.0	5.6	8.7	565	880
	2300	48	94	3.7	6.0	9.4	565	885
	2200	45	89	3.6	6.3	9.8	562	875
12,500	2650	63	117	4.7	4.8	7.4	555	860
	2600	60	113	4.5	5.0	7.7	560	875
	2500	55	105	4.2	5.4	8.4	570	885
	2400	51	99	3.9	5.8	9.0	570	890
	2300	48	89	3.7	6.1	9.5	545	845

NOTES: 1. Maximum cruise is normally limited to 75% power.
2. In the above calculations of endurance in hours and range in miles, no allowances were made for take-off or reserve.
3. Cruise and range performance figures shown are applicable to the COMMUTER. For the STANDARD and TRAINER versions, subtract 2 MPH from the higher cruise speeds and 1 MPH from the lower cruise speeds shown.

Figure 5-4.

MAXIMUM GLIDE
• SPEED 65 MPH (IAS)
• PROPELLER WINDMILLING
• FLAPS UP • ZERO WIND
HEIGHT ABOVE TERRAIN (FEET)
12,000
10,000
8000
6000
4000
2000
0
0
5
10
15
20
GROUND DISTANCE (STATUTE MILES)

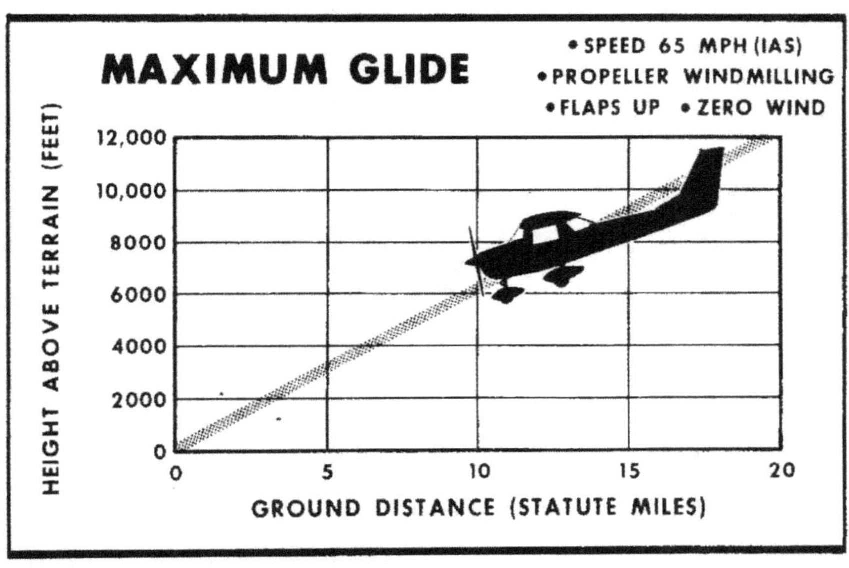

Figure 5-5.

OPTIONAL SYSTEMS

This section contains a description, operating procedures, and performance data (when applicable) for some of the optional equipment which may be installed in your Cessna. Owner's Manual Supplements are provided to cover operation of other optional equipment systems when installed in your airplane. Contact your Cessna Dealer for a complete list of available optional equipment.

LONG RANGE FUEL TANKS

Special wings with long range fuel tanks are available to replace the standard wings and fuel tanks for greater endurance and range. Each tank has a total capacity of 19 gallons. Usable fuel in each long range tank, for all flight conditions, is 17.5 gallons.

COLD WEATHER EQUIPMENT

WINTERIZATION KIT.

For continuous operation in temperatures consistently below 20° F, the Cessna winterization kit, available from your Cessna Dealer, should be installed to improve engine operation.

RADIO TRANSMITTER SELECTOR SWITCH

Operation of the radio equipment is normal as covered in the respective radio manuals. When more than one radio with transmitter function is installed, a transmitter switch is necessary. The transmitter selector switch is mounted in the upper left corner of the control pedestal and has two positions. When two transmitters are installed, it is necessary to switch the microphone to the radio unit the pilot desires to use for transmission. This is accomplished by placing the transmitter selector switch in the position corresponding to the radio unit which is to be used.

TRUE AIRSPEED INDICATOR

The airspeed indicator, installed in the Model 150, can be converted to a true airspeed indicator by the addition of a calibrated ring and bezel to the front face of the instrument. The rotatable ring works in conjunction with the airspeed indicator dial in a manner similar to the operation of a flight computer.

TO OBTAIN TRUE AIRSPEED, rotate ring until pressure altitude is aligned with outside air temperature in degrees Fahrenheit. Then read true airspeed on rotatable ring opposite airspeed needle.

NOTE

Pressure altitude should not be confused with indicated altitude. To obtain pressure altitude, set barometric scale on altimeter to "29.92" and read pressure altitude opposite needle on altimeter. Be sure to return altimeter barometric scale to original barometric setting after pressure altitude has been obtained.

ALPHABETICAL INDEX

A

After Landing, 1-3
Air Filter, Carburetor, 4-7
Air Filter, Gyro Instrument, 4-7
Air Filter, Vacuum System, 4-7
Airplane,
    before entering, 1-1
    file, 4-5
    ground handling, 4-1
    mooring, 4-1
    secure, 1-4
Airspeed Correction Table, 5-2
Airspeed Limitations, 3-2
Aluminum Surfaces, 4-3
Authorized Operations, 3-1

B

Baggage, Capacity, inside cover
Baggage Loading/Tie-Down, 3-4
Battery, 4-7
Beacon, Rotating, 2-3
Before Entering the Airplane, 1-1
Before Landing, 1-3
Before Starting the Engine, 1-1
Before Take-Off, 1-2, 2-6
    magneto check, 2-6
    warm-up, 2-6
Brake Master Cylinders, 4-7
Brake System, Parking, 2-4

C

Cabin Heating and Ventilating
  System, 2-4

Capacity,
    baggage, inside cover
    fuel, inside covers
    oil, inside covers
Carburetor, 2-2
    air filter, 4-7
Care,
    exterior, 4-2, 4-3
    interior, 4-3
    propeller, 4-3
Center of Gravity Moment
  Envelope, 3-6
Check List, Servicing Intervals, 4-7
Climb, 1-3, 2-8
    climb data, 2-8
    climb speeds, 2-8
    go-around climb, 2-8
    maximum performance, 1-3
    maximum rate-of-climb data,
      5-3
    normal, 1-3
Cold Weather Equipment, 6-1
    winterization kit, 6-1
Cold Weather Operation, 2-10
Correction Table, Airspeed, 5-2
Crosswind Landing, 2-9
Crosswind, Take-Off, 2-7
Cruise Performance, Optimum, 2-9
Cruise Performance Table, 5-4
Cruising, 1-3, 2-8

D

Diagram,
    baggage loading/tie-down, 3-4
    exterior inspection, iv
    maximum glide, 5-5

SERVICING REQUIREMENTS

FUEL:

      AVIATION GRADE -- 80/87 MINIMUM GRADE
      CAPACITY EACH STANDARD TANK -- 13 GALLONS
      CAPACITY EACH LONG RANGE TANK -- 19 GALLONS

ENGINE OIL:

      AVIATION GRADE -- SAE 20 BELOW 40° F.
                       SAE 40 ABOVE 40° F.
      (AIRCRAFT DELIVERED WITH STRAIGHT MINERAL
      OIL. EITHER MINERAL OIL OR DETERGENT OIL
      MAY BE USED. IF DETERGENT OIL IS USED, IT
      MUST CONFORM TO CONTINENTAL MOTORS
      SPECIFICATION MHS-24.)
      CAPACITY OF ENGINE SUMP -- 6 QUARTS
      (DO NOT OPERATE ON LESS THAN 4 QUARTS. TO
      MINIMIZE LOSS OF OIL THROUGH BREATHER, FILL
      TO 5 QUART LEVEL FOR NORMAL FLIGHTS OF LESS
      THAN 3 HOURS. FOR EXTENDED FLIGHT, FILL TO
      6 QUARTS. IF OPTIONAL OIL FILTER IS INSTALLED,
      ONE ADDITIONAL QUART IS REQUIRED WHEN THE
      FILTER ELEMENT IS CHANGED.

HYDRAULIC FLUID:

      MIL-H-5606 HYDRAULIC FLUID

TIRE PRESSURE:

      NOSE WHEEL --- 30 PSI ON 5:00 × 5 TIRE
                    21 PSI ON 6:00 × 6 TIRE (OPT)
      MAIN WHEELS -- 21 PSI ON 6:00 × 6 TIRES